Introducing Continents

North America

Chris Oxlade

Heinemann
LIBRARY

Chicago, Illinois

© 2014 Heinemann Library
an imprint of Capstone Global Library, LLC
Chicago, Illinois

To contact Capstone Global Library please phone 800-747-4992, or visit our web site, www.capstonepub.com

Edited by Dan Nunn, Rebecca Rissman, Sian Smith, and Helen Cox Cannons
Designed by Philippa Jenkins
Original illustrations © Capstone Global Library Ltd 2014
Picture research by Liz Alexander and Tristan Leverett
Production by Vicki Fitzgerald
Originated by Capstone Global Library Ltd

Library of Congress Cataloging-in-Publication Data
Oxlade, Chris.

Introducing North America / Chris Oxlade.

pages cm.—(Introducing continents)

Includes bibliographical references and index.

ISBN 978-1-4329-8043-6 (hb)—ISBN 978-1-4329-8051-1 (pb) 1. North America—Juvenile literature. I. Title.

E38.5.O97 2013
970—dc23   2012049497

Acknowledgments
The author and publisher are grateful to the following for permission to reproduce copyright material: Getty Images: Ingram Publishing, 17, John A. Rizzo, 19, Rick Gerharter /Lonely Planet Images, 11, Robyn Beck/AFP, 13, Stephen Brashear, 27, Susana Gonzalez/Bloomberg, 26, Tim Graham, 21, Wayne R Bilenduke, 18; Science Source: JEFFREY LEPORE, 14; Shutterstock: aceshot1, 20, Anton Foltin, 16, AridOcean, Cover (map), Bryan Busovicki, 6, Gail Johnson, 8, Kamira, 23, kavram, 9, markrhiggins, 15, S.Borisov, 24, somchaij, Cover Top; SuperStock: age fotostock, Cover Bottom, 7, Design Pics, 10, Jeff Schultz/Alaska Stock, 12, Susan E. Pease/age fotostock, 25.

Printed in the United States   6062

Contents

Some words are shown in bold, **like this**. You can find out what they mean by looking in the glossary.

About North America

North America is one of the world's seven **continents**. A continent is a huge area of land. North America is the third largest continent. It stretches almost from the **equator** in the south to the **Arctic** in the north.

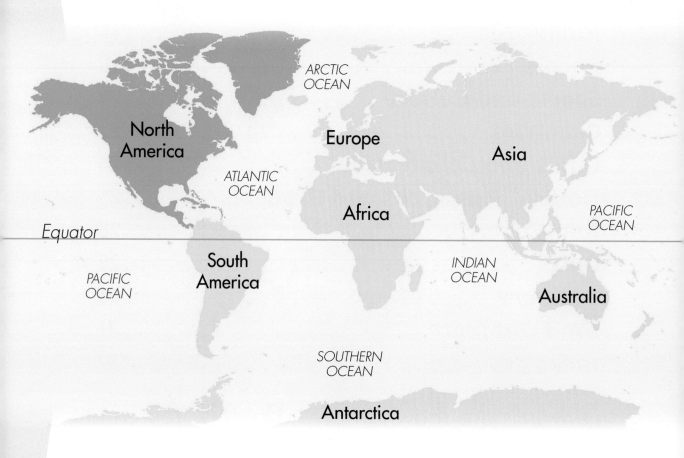

ARCTIC
OCEAN

North
America

Europe

Asia

ATLANTIC
OCEAN

Africa

PACIFIC
OCEAN

Equator

PACIFIC
OCEAN

South
America

INDIAN
OCEAN

Australia

SOUTHERN
OCEAN

Antarctica

North America sits between the Atlantic Ocean in the east and the Pacific Ocean in the west. North America is connected to the continent of South America by a narrow strip of land. This area is called Central America.

North America Fact File	
Area	9,456,000 square miles (24,490,000 square kilometers)
Population	542 million
Number of countries	23
Highest mountain	Mount McKinley at 20,322 feet (6,194 meters)
Longest river	Missouri at 2,341 miles (3,768 kilometers)

Famous Places

There are many amazing natural landmarks in North America. The Grand Canyon in Arizona, in the United States, is 277 miles (445 kilometers) long. Niagara Falls and Yellowstone National Park are also popular places to visit.

In some places, the Grand Canyon is 1 mile (1.6 kilometers) deep.

This is the Pyramid of the Niches in the ancient city of El Tajin in Mexico.

There are many famous buildings too. In Mexico, there are pyramids built about 500 years ago by people called the Aztecs. Modern buildings include the CN Tower in Toronto, Canada, and the Hoover Dam in the United States.

Geography

The largest **mountain range** in North America is the Rocky Mountains, in the west. The Rockies stretch almost 3,100 miles (5,000 kilometers) from Mexico to Alaska. The Appalachian Mountains are on the east side of North America.

Coast Mountains

Rocky Mountains

Great Basin

Death Valley

Sonoran Desert

Mojave Desert

Chihuahuan Desert

Appalachian Mountains

Sierra Madre Occidental

Sierra Madre Oriental

| 0 | 500 miles |
| 0 | 800 km |

Mount McKinley, in Alaska, is the highest mountain in North America.

This part of the Mojave Desert is called Death Valley because it is so hot and dry.

There are **deserts** in the southwest of North America. They include the Mojave Desert in California and the Sonoran Desert in New Mexico. The Great **Plains** is a huge area of flat land in the center of North America. It is also called the **prairie**.

There are five huge lakes along the border between the United States and Canada. They are called the Great Lakes. Lake Superior is one of the Great Lakes. It is the world's largest **freshwater** lake.

This photograph shows Lake Superior in winter.

Yukon River

Mackenzie River

Columbia River

Lake Superior St. Lawrence River

Mississippi River

Missouri River

Colorado River

Ohio River

Hudson River

The Great Lakes

Rio Grande

0	500 miles
0	800 km

This paddle steamer is taking tourists on a trip along the Mississippi.

The Missouri is the longest river in North America. It is 2,341 miles (3,768 kilometers) long. It flows across the center of the United States and into the Mississippi River. The St. Lawrence River connects the Great Lakes with the Atlantic Ocean.

Weather

North America has many different types of weather. In the south, it is tropical. This means it is hot and there is lots of rain. In the north, it is very cold year-round, and there is lots of snow.

In the far north of North America, there are times during the winter when it stays dark all day.

Hurricane Rita caused this flooding in Louisiana, in the United States.

Extreme weather sometimes strikes North America. **Hurricanes** are giant storms. They bring powerful winds and heavy rains to Central America, the Caribbean, and the southeast United States. **Tornadoes** also hit the United States.

Animals

An amazing variety of animals live in North America. Polar bears live in the far north, and grizzly bears live in the forests and mountains farther south. Bison live on the **plains**. They are also known as buffalo.

This grizzly bear is living high in the Rocky Mountains.

Alligators live in swamps called the Everglades in Florida.

Alligators live in lakes, rivers, and **swamps** in the southeast United States. Hundreds of different types of birds make their homes in the rain forests of Central America. Jaguars live in the rain forests too.

Plants

A giant plant grows in the **deserts** in the south of North America. It is the saguaro cactus. It grows up to 49 feet (15 meters) high. It survives on very little water.

These saguaro cactuses are growing in the desert in Arizona.

These enormous trees are giant redwoods.

There are vast conifer forests in the north of North America. Conifer trees stay green year-round. Giant redwood trees grow there too. They are the tallest trees in the world. They grow up to 367 feet (112 meters) high!

People

American Indians were the first people to live in North America. There are many groups of American Indians all over North America. People from all over Europe settled in North America too, including from Britain, France, and Spain.

Inuit people live in the far north of North America.

People from many different groups live in New York City.

Most people in the United States speak English. Many people in Central America and Mexico speak Spanish, and many people in Canada speak French. American Indians often speak their own languages.

Sports and Culture

Baseball, basketball, and ice hockey are popular sports in the United States and Canada. Football began in the United States. The Super Bowl is the biggest game of the year.

This crowd is enjoying a Cincinnati Reds baseball game.

This reggae band is playing on the island of Jamaica.

Hollywood is in Los Angeles, California. It is the center of the movie industry in the United States. Hundreds of movies are made there every year. Popular music in North America includes country music in the United States and reggae music in the islands of the Caribbean.

Countries

There are 23 countries in North America. The **continent** is made up mostly of three very large countries. These are the United States of America (USA), Canada, and Mexico. Canada is the second largest country in the world, after Russia.

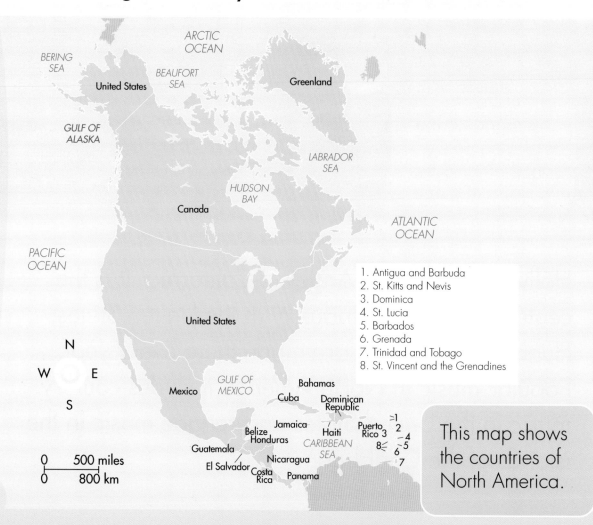

1. Antigua and Barbuda
2. St. Kitts and Nevis
3. Dominica
4. St. Lucia
5. Barbados
6. Grenada
7. Trinidad and Tobago
8. St. Vincent and the Grenadines

This map shows the countries of North America.

This is a street in Havana, the capital city of Cuba.

Most of the countries of North America are islands in the Caribbean Sea, such as Cuba and Jamaica. Greenland is the world's largest island, but it is not a country. It is part of Denmark, a country in Europe.

Cities and Countryside

New York City, Los Angeles, Mexico City, and Toronto are some of the cities in North America with the greatest number of people. Mexico City is the largest city in North America. Around 20 million people live there. New York is an important world business center.

There are dozens of skyscrapers in the center of New York City.

This is the main street in April, a town in Massachusetts.

There are thousands of small towns in the **plains** of North America. Many people who live there are farmers who grow wheat and raise cattle. In Central America, most people work on small farms. They grow coffee, sugar, or bananas.

Natural Resources and Products

Trees are cut down in the forests of Canada and the United States. The wood is used to make furniture, houses, and many other wooden objects. Oil and gas are found under the ground and ocean in many places.

This oil rig is in the Gulf of Mexico.

Boeing airplanes are made in this giant factory.

North America has many different industries. Cars are made in the United States, Canada, and Mexico. Boeing airplanes are made near Seattle, Washington. Silicon Valley in California is the home of the U.S. computer industry.

Fun Facts

- The Panama Canal cuts through the middle of the country of Panama. It carries huge ships between the Atlantic Ocean and the Pacific Ocean.

- Tornado Alley is an area in the center of the United States where many **tornadoes** hit every year.

- Greenland is covered with a sheet of ice that is almost 2 miles (3 kilometers) thick in some places.

- The Boeing aircraft factory near Seattle, Washington, is the world's largest building.

Quiz

1. Which part of North America is the biggest island in the world?

2. What is the largest mountain range in North America?

3. Who built pyramids in Mexico?

4. What is the world's largest freshwater lake?

4. Lake Superior

3. The Aztecs

2. The Rocky Mountains in the United States

1. Greenland

Glossary

Arctic area of Earth around the North Pole, where it is always cold

continent one of seven huge areas of land on Earth

desert area of land that gets very little rain

equator imaginary line running around the middle of Earth

freshwater water that fills rivers and lakes. It is not salty like ocean water.

hurricane fierce storm that brings strong winds and heavy rain

mountain range long line of mountains

plains flat lands

prairie huge area of grassland or farmland

swamps places where the ground is muddy or flooded

tornado spinning column of air that brings very strong winds

Find Out More

Books

Binns, Tristan Boyer. *Exploring North America.* Chicago: Heinemann, 2007.

Gibson, Karen Bush. *Spotlight on North America.* Mankato, Minn.: Capstone, 2011.

Royston, Angela and Michael Scott. *North America's Most Amazing Plants.* Chicago: Raintree, 2009.

Web sites

FactHound offers a safe, fun way to find Internet sites related to this book. All of the sites on FactHound have been researched by our staff.

Here's all you do:
Visit www.facthound.com
Type in this code: 9781432980436

Index